Also by Robert A Kandarjian

Sacred Intentions

Life and Afterlife, Q & A

Dear Diana

thank you for

generously sharing

your Light.

R.

10/17/2010

# THE MASCULINE HEART

## What makes men tick

Robert A Kandarjian

iUniverse, Inc.
New York   Bloomington

iUniverse books may be ordered through booksellers or by contacting:

iUniverse
1663 Liberty Drive
Bloomington, IN 47403
www.iuniverse.com
1-800-Authors (1-800-288-4677)

Because of the dynamic nature of the Internet, any Web addresses or links contained in this book may have changed since publication and may no longer be valid. The views expressed in this work are solely those of the author and do not necessarily reflect the views of the publisher, and the publisher hereby disclaims any responsibility for them.

ISBN: 978-1-4502-4867-9 (sc)
ISBN: 978-1-4502-4869-3 (ebook)

Printed in the United States of America

Photo by: Dominique Perez

iUniverse rev. date: 08/18/2010

*Dedicated to our brave
and tender boyhood*

# Contents

# Acknowledgement

I am deeply grateful to all those patients, both men and women, whose stories and accounts about the male heart have expanded my awareness and understanding of men's issues. I remain humbled by their personal conflicts and search for truth and regard them as my teachers.

I am grateful to the following colleagues and friends who have for years graciously afforded me invaluable discussions on the subject of men: Anthony Santore DC, Emmanuel Hriso MD, Meliné Karakashian, PhD., Mr. Karen Ambartsoumean, Sheila Pearl MSW, Diana Kalfayan MSW, Seta Shahinian, Amy Rozen LCH, Indira Darst R.N., Jean Marie Rosone MSW, Rachel Gates, Angela Vanario, Stephen Bryant, and of course my brother Vahe. From those discussions I've gained a deeper understanding about the challenges we men face, and on a personal note, a greater clarity about my personal healing process. I thank a trio of talent and power: Debbie Peterson for your inexhaustible support in moving this manuscript to print, Jennifer Comras for your laser beam focus and sage advice, and Deana Valente for your caring guidance and cheerleading enthusiasm.

I thank my childhood buddies who have taught me bravery, humility and joy. I want to especially acknowledge and thank my family for their enduring love, patience and support throughout my life; their consistent affection for me has been and remains the anchor from which I draw lessons, purpose, and joy.

# Preface: Father and son

To any little kid growing up in one of the "undesirable" neighborhoods of Beirut in the 50s and 60s, the stench of poverty and injustice was a detectable odor that hovered over the streets and permeated the soft faces of the innocent. It was all very loud, very boisterous, in your face, a take it or leave it quarter where most kids would inevitably abandon sweetness to some cursed dimension and reluctantly adjust to a daily rhythm of despair and violence. I never went back since I left that place at fourteen, and more often than I would like to admit, resented my father for not getting us all out of there sooner. I wanted him to rescue us, be my hero, but I did not know his story. I wanted so desperately to know his story but he buried it with him on a sunny October day in 1989. I wanted to know his story so we could feel something permanent, radiant, so I could anchor and construct my male story. Instead, what we inevitably constructed between us was a painfully recognized distance, a fracture.

He had physically survived the Armenian Genocide as a little boy but had not escaped the psychic wounds of that horror. He did his best as most fathers do, but he would not or could not tell his tale to his children. His tale was deeply buried and I believe he felt it must remain buried in order to protect his children from the dark forces that had killed his father, all the men in his family, and most of the Armenian inhabitants of his town. Lebanon was a lesser hell to him than his childhood town in Eastern Anatolia so why was I complaining? The mixture of feelings about the dangerous alleys of Beirut and an inaccessible father gradually evaporated my childhood bliss and stirred to surface my probing whys. Why the madness on the streets, the numbness, the silence, the fracture? Why became my comforter, redeemer and best friend. If I could answer the whys I can reclaim my aliveness, my father, my story, and thus move forward. But children can't move forward when their storytellers have sealed their lips. Yes, many who knew my father would attest to his very few words, but when one paid careful attention, one could detect in his gentle and mild-mannered deeds the call to selfless action. His heart wanted the world to burst open and invite goodness and mercy because he had known and lived their opposites.

This book could not have materialized if it wasn't for my Lebanese years and if I wasn't the son of a silent storyteller. This book is his voice and perhaps the end of his silence, and I trust the end of our fracture as father and son. I thank my childhood alleys and streets and am eternally grateful to my Baba, who resides safely in the sanctuary of God's grace.

# Introduction

After much storytelling, guidance and training from his father, grandfathers and uncles, the male hero in legendary stories and myths leaves the nest of his loving mother and the comforts of his home to embark upon his journey into manhood. He tackles down beasts and overcomes challenges and through his adventures discovers his capacity for courage and bravery and quickly learns to respect and honor the visible and invisible forces of the Earth and the Sky. As his journey progresses, the boy learns to maneuver between actions and emotions of guts and humility, valor and mercy, and eventually holds in possession and expression the *fullness* of his feelings, purpose, mission and essence inside a man's body. I understand and appreciate this journey of the hero as a process with a twofold task: an inner task of the male to seek and possess the above fullness that is his masculine right, and an outer task to contribute the wisdom of this fullness to the tribe and to the world at large.

The legends and myths of the male hero are in essence stories about self-possession and contribution. Self-possessed men, rather than men who are possessed by external forces, possess the following: Their emotions in full spectrum, the instinctual-intuitive self, the reasoning-intellectual mind, the creative-spiritual self, drive and direction; moreover, they possess the ability to see the bigger picture and contribute to the higher good.

In a consumer culture where the party line thinking is "more profits," it becomes impossible for most men to feel their heroic pulse and their sacred self-possession when they are regarded mainly as buyers and end users. And in our pervasive atmosphere of competition that repeatedly supplants cooperation, it is difficult to feel connected in a brotherly fashion to our fellow men and deliver *real and lasting* contributions. The masculine heart as grandfather, father, son, brother and uncle is in trouble and has been for some time. Our male journey for self-possession and contribution has turned out to be a failed one; we've allowed the cant of corporate, Hollywood-Madison Avenue cultures replace the fathers, the grandfathers and uncles and succeed as the all encompassing primary storytellers. We must acknowledge that most of our boys today don't reach adulthood in possession and expression of the *fullness* of their feelings, purpose, mission and essence; the free markets continue to win and take possession. Fathers who want to be and should be their boys' primary storyteller will have to challenge and dethrone the Goliath storytellers driven by profiteering motives. With the power of their paternal love and instincts, fathers must fight and rescue their boys from the seduction and glamour of materialism and bring down the false prophets who are determined to serve profits and not our boys.

To blame only genetics and poor parenting for the troubles we men create for ourselves and each other is quite naïve. Like parts of a body, psychology, economics, science, politics, arts and spirituality are all interlaced components of the whole; the micro and the macro interface and affect each other daily. Parents don't operate in a vacuum; parents as well as culture shape children and future parents. As much as he tries, modern man can not fully repossess his self through the employment of valuable psychotherapy and constructive self-help tools in an environment where the powerful continue to abuse power by designing rules that undermine and demoralize the male spirit. We are living within an underhanded cultural complex whose leaders have allowed the masculine heart to be chipped away by policies that place profits before people. It is cruel and unjust to expect the average man to "cope" with the pressures of daily life when those pressures are a result of a leadership that robs men of their manhood and denies them an equitable social safety net. Today's man is not tackling eye-catching lions and tigers like his ancestors, but a more formidable rival insulated in steel and glass towers beyond reach. For decades, unfair social and economic policies on housing, education, environment, food and healthcare by unaccountable and unregulated authorities have deeply wounded the masculine heart and have unleashed nightmares inside family nests. The individual man can not heal his heart in such a landscape of contamination. The individual is a product of the community and the community a responsible steward of the individual; the two are one and inseparable. So, success must be redefined by a new generation of men and I hope this book can contribute to such discourse and plant seeds that can help us all find our lost power and goodness as men so the future credo can shift to *people before profits*. The male story of self-possession and contribution must unfold and movers and shakers must move into their hearts and reside within it. The time is ripe. We need shepherds who don't beat us up and kick us when we're down; but rather, lead us with a spiritual mercy that is respectful of the visible and invisible forces of the Earth and the Sky.

# PART ONE

# Terror

*Nearly all men can stand adversity, but if you want to test a man's character, give him power.*

*Abraham Lincoln*

## Lost

Yes we men aren't very good at asking for directions when lost on the road. And now that we have our sexy GPS mistresses on our dashboards we don't have to, we're doing just fine thank you very much. Nevertheless, below is a laundry list of conscious and unconscious monologues that run through our heads and hearts when we think about asking for directions or when we are forced to ask for directions by fellow passengers.

They'll screw me and give me wrong directions.
I don't need anybody's help.
My dad never asked for help.
I know where I'm going.
I don't want to waste time.
I don't want to be told what to do.
I know what I'm doing.
Don't worry everyone, I'm in control.
I can do it on my own.
I don't trust anyone's directions.
I don't need your help.
I'm supposed to do it alone.
I should be able to do it alone.
I feel small when I ask for help.
It's humiliating to ask for help.
I look stupid asking for directions.
I'll look incompetent.

Only losers ask for help.
I'll be laughed at.
Don't show them you don't know.
Well, I never considered asking for direction.
I'm scared to ask for help.

There is more but thanks for reading this short list.

＊

## A letter from Joe

Parker famly

i know itis tough fr you to fugive me, mabe imposable.
but i got to tel you somethin you know im servin 33 yer
sentenc fr takin yur kids life when i was 28. im naw 53.
last cople yers i been feelin bad bout the hole thing. took
me ovr 25 yers in this waysteland to start feelin bad bout
sometin. mabe it was no waysteland, mabe all them yers
was not a wayste. i can feel bad about yur kid. i feel bad
about sometin, bout yur kid. i shuldnt not done it. itwas
a stupid thing to do. the minster sayz im feelin remose.
i guess if you dont furgive me it dont mater. this remose
thing is good fr me, good now. i just gut to furgive myself,
thats ma job. hope you read this. Joe P.

im Joes sellmat my name Larry. i rite ths letter for Joe
cause he dont know how to rite. he want to lern.
Godbye

✳

## Note 1

**Ter-ror** (ter'er) *noun.* Intense overpowering fear. Anything that instills such a fear; a terrifying object or occurrence. The ability to instill such a fear. Violence toward private citizens, public property and political enemies prompted by a political group to achieve or maintain supremacy. Middle English *terrour,* from Old French, from Latin *terror,* from *terrere,* to frighten.

**Remorse** is overly underrated while shopping, buying, consuming, accumulating, accruing, collecting and hoarding overrated. Remorse, for a lack of better word, is good; in fact, it is great. Too bad we don't promote it as successfully as we promote greed. Once we know someone's remorse is genuine, authentic, real, really real, we need to open dialogue without forgetting their past actions. Forgiving someone who has violated you can take years. If they remain in denial about violating you, massacring your ancestors and polluting the planet, pray for them please. Pray and ask Mr. & Mrs. Mercy to connect them to their purity. They may appear to enjoy their morning stroll but they are in pain, deep soul pain because you can't destroy a planet, hurt or kill a human, without destroying, hurting or killing a piece of you. Ask any soldier in a moment of true reflection what happened to him when he killed and you'll see his chest deflate, his eyes fill up and his spirit collapse. On his deathbed as he is vacating his precious body, he will enter and exit that delirious territory of remorse wishing and wanting absolution. His commander may give him a hundred reasons why he had to kill but ultimately it is he, the dying soldier, who has to reclaim and rescue that piece in him that feels dead.

Because the environment most of us men live in promotes denial and distraction and does not support our journey toward remorse, many of us get busy pumping and businessing and sidestep remorse. In order to feel remorse, one must remain silent and lie in the arms of a wise merciful friend. From that silence will eventually bellow a voice, *"How could I have done that, what on earth was I thinking when I did that? When I exploited nine-year old children in my factory, when I dumped you know what in the Mississippi, when I planted landmines in fields, when I lied for my boss, when I, when I, I can't bare it anymore, I can't speak of the unspeakable."* When remorse envelops the body from within and without it makes room for self-forgiveness and redemption. When a child mourns the death of his pet turtle because he forgot to feed it, he learns accountability.

Then there are men who can't feel remorse, at least not in this lifetime. They don't get we are wired to connect and that every purchase and sale we make from bread, butter, bullets and beans effects the other side of the planet. Because these souls are deeply disconnected from your vulnerability and mine they can't understand why you're complaining, why you're so gloomy. But men who can't feel remorse feel a desperate but well-hidden sac of fears: Fear of betraying the clan, fear of not belonging, fear of looking like a wimp, fear of losing face, fear of disapproval, fear of rejection and exile, fear of fear. It's no easy thing to live with an inventory of such fears and pretend you don't feel them. We must have pity for the childhood of remorseless beings because they suffered a great and desperate tragedy. They were asked to; no, they were forced to abandon their softness, their vulnerability, their mercy. In order to survive their childhood, they built an armored chest that they fortified year after year. Let's pray they overcome their fears and terrors and feel courageous enough to be silent in the arms of the wise merciful friend. Their soul did not want to be this, this tragedy, this disaster, this remorseless thing. Deep down, their soul wanted to connect, contribute, and feed the turtle.

✳

## Will # 1

Will: Listen doc, my hands shake and my sleep is miserable. Jack's the best neurologist this side of the Mississippi and told me nothing is wrong from his end so he referred me to you. No disrespect to your profession, but if it wasn't for my wife I wouldn't be here. I'm having trouble working. I hate to admit it but I'm just not solid. Maybe you have a medication that can help.

Dr. Hassan: There might be. Let's explore a bit and see what started all this.

Will: I did that with Jack. CT, MRI, you name it, he couldn't find a thing.

Dr. Hassan: Mr. Franklin you are 68 and you work 60 to 70 hours a week. Dr. Forster's report strongly suggested that you slow things down.

Will: I have.

Dr. Hassan: Doesn't seem you have succeeded according to what you told me earlier. I don't think medications alone will help you.

Will: But Jack said you could help.

Dr. Hassan: I need your help to do that Mr. Franklin.

Will: Isn't there something you can prescribe?

Dr. Hassan: Not without some background and your promise to slow things down.

Will: My wife's going to send you roses.

Dr. Hassan: She must care about you a great deal.

Will: She does.

Dr. Hassan: Your work, it means a lot to you.

Will: My work?

Dr. Hassan: Yes, your work.

Will: It does. It's everything besides my family.

Dr. Hassan: Tell me about yourself a little.

Will: I grew up in Virginia, college and then law school. Worked in England for six years where I met my wife and got married. Moved to Maryland with her at 33 and I've been here ever since. I have a firm in DC with two partners and I'm on the board of two companies and a local hospital.

I have three kids, my oldest, a girl, a firecracker, works with me and my youngest is a lobbyist.

Dr. Hassan: Your middle one?

Will: Joey, thirty-one, two degrees and still lost. How's all this related to my condition?

Dr. Hassan: I don't know yet Mr. Franklin. We're trying to find out. Can you tell me about your work?

Will: Not much to tell.

Dr. Hassan: What's the biggest stressor in your life?

Will: Getting old.

Dr. Hassan: Are your parents still living?

Will: No

Dr. Hassan: Do you have siblings?

Will: I had a younger brother who was killed by a drunken driver and one older sister.

Dr. Hassan: How old were you when your brother died.

Will: He didn't die. He was killed. I was seventeen. Why the history?

Dr. Hassan: You are highly regarded in your profession I understand. Do you enjoy that admiration, respect?

Will: I get the job done and I certainly have my critics.

Dr. Hassan: Does that hurt you, the critics, does it effect you negatively?

Will: I don't give a hoot as long as I get the job done.

Dr. Hassan: It's important for you to get the job done.

Will: That's what I get paid for, like you, you get paid to get the job done.

Dr. Hassan: Is anyone in your family affected negatively by the critics?

Will: My wife sometimes but she's a rock, always on my side.

Dr. Hassan: Who's not on your side?

Will: When you're a corporate tax attorney, a lot of folks.

Dr. Hassan: And the kids, they're on your side?

Will: They're not kids anymore. My middle one could toughen up a bit.

Dr. Hassan: How so?

Will: How's this connected to my hands, my sleep?

Dr. Hassan: We're trying to find out.

Will: We're wasting time.

Dr. Hassan: I don't think so Mr. Franklin.

Will: I do.

Dr. Hassan: If you feel we're wasting time you can return to Dr. Forster and I'll send him my report.

Will: I might do that.

✳

## Note 2

**If** you get a chance, a lucky chance, to sit with a hard core criminal or a merciless CEO who feel safe enough to tell you their *whole* story, you'll get a solid education on how to prevent heartbreak and quickly learn that heartbreak doesn't happen in a vacuum, it takes a *whole* village to create it. White collar, blue collar, high collar and no collar criminals, they're all prisoners of childhood. For now jail is a good place for them to cool off until one day, one fine day, one promised blessed day, we all wake up to the apparent plain in sight solution and stop depriving our boys their basic need. What they need and what they have always needed and what they will continue to need for the next million years is merciful nurturing and guidance of their sweet hearts and soul. Ultimately we men are here to recognize, sense, and feel in our blood and bones that separation is illusion, that separation from our brothers and sisters and separation from the full spectrum of our emotions is mental, physical and global breakdown. That day, that month or that year *will* come when we are knocked down to our knees and the hard shell that once housed our well hidden fears and stubborn male pride is cracked open. Call it "The Humbling." After the breakdown will come the breakthrough, the realization that perhaps we were too arrogant, too greedy, too serious, too passive, too responsible, ungrateful, irresponsible, too scared, too naïve, unspiritual, evil. We don't have to grow through breakdowns and crises anymore when we can grow through watchful and mindful awareness. Awareness means talking real stuff with our buddies, therapy (not all therapists are good), silence, how to books, time alone, time with a safe and wise friend, your pet, a diary, or anything that opens our heart and mind to the world and to our male goodness.

What do you think happens to boys who are hurt over and over again because their physical space was violated, their need for male mirroring deprived, their need for comfort shunned, their lovely voices overpowered and their little will crushed? If they still have any life-force left in them and haven't become social anomalies frozen in terror, they get frustrated and angry. What do you think happens when they don't have permission to express that frustration and anger? *"Get out of my face and don't you raise your voice, you have no right no right to talk to me like that, you hold your tongue you hear?"* So here you are a kid walking around all alone with all this hurt and held anger that over the years brew into depression and rage to a point where you no longer remember how to articulate your feelings into words. Your hurt goes from frustration to anger to rage and as you get older the rage boils over into fury and murderous rage. What do you do with all this fire, all this betrayal, where do you put it, how do you process it, how do you safely discharge it? Under the fire is hurt. Under the fire are the hidden tears of a neglected shivering body of a boy. Slow down the fire and you'll feel the shiver - scary, cold. *"Don't you go start cryin cause that's gonna get you nowhere boy, now go to your room and shut."* You go to your room and force yourself to not be angry, to not be a coward and cry; you force yourself to put out the fire, to be a good boy, to hold it all together, to not crack, to hold it all in. But how long can you hold it all in? Now you're a man who is a good boy, a very good bureaucrat and corporate employee who obeys rules and follows orders even when they don't make sense, who passively says yes to things he should say no to, who dares not make waves. You stay a good boy and thank goodness you hold it all in and hide your dark side, that side of you that could explode and really hurt someone. But you can't forever hide your dark side and bury all that fire and betrayal, all that anger, sorrow and rage you felt in your bedroom decades ago, it can't be done. It leaks out in self-betrayal, self-hate, exploitation, self-exploitation, abuse, self-abuse, prejudice, child abuse, violence, suicide, and road-rage. It leaks out in the workplace with ninety-hour work weeks and cutthroat competition. And much too often, the darkness leaks out from the bedroom to the boardroom as your oblivious greed signs papers that devastate lives, a greed that grants you your temporary high, a fix awaiting downfall.

The nature of our biology is such that we can't bury anger, sorrow, rage, fear and hurt; the body can't hold them in forever. The fire will fire out sooner or later, if not in abuse of power then in a physical meltdown, a mental breakdown, an addiction, a diagnosis. The body can't house and accommodate such fiery emotions for decades and generations without something breaking and giving way to tragedy. So how do we prevent boys from becoming uncaring parents, ruthless (ruth means pity, mercy, compassion, sympathy, remorse) CEOs and brutal leaders? Beneath every boy's anger is fear and hurt and he is angry because no one is addressing the fear and the hurt. When he's speaking from the fear and the hurt and nobody is listening he gets frustrated. If he continues speaking from the fear and the hurt and still nobody listens, he gets angry, *"I'm not gonna hear it you useless piece of nothin, now get out of my face and stop lookin at me like that."* So you're a nothing, invisible, you don't matter, you don't exist. Anger if unresolved will usually escalate to rage. You've heard about those so called bad kids who bully other kids and who torture and kill insects and animals for fun. These are a group of very very hurt, angry and sorrowful kids with very very deep fears and terrors, the deepest being the terror of opening their hearts, *again*. These are the "bad boys" who will very likely be the next generation of sociopaths and psychopaths and if they rise to positions of economic and political power (which many have and many more will), you and I will have to do lot more praying. Dig into the childhood of infamous dictators, ruthless CEOs and serial killers and you'll find a common denominator: Terrorized children who did not have permission to express their legitimate fears and hurt. *"Yea I slashed that sucker and it felt good, damn good."*

✳

## Will # 2

Dr Hassan: So where did you go to receive comfort, to feel comforted when you were growing up, whom did you turn to?

Will: I don't remember. My horse Killian I suppose.

Dr Hassan: Were there any adults that you remember that you may have turned to for comfort?

Will: I don't think so.

Dr. Hassan: And your wife?

Will: Meaning?

Dr. Hassan: Do you turn to her for comfort?

Will: She doesn't need to know my troubles.

Dr. Hassan: Why not?

Will: I want Jenny to focus on the house, the kids.

Dr. Hassan: Not on you?

Will: No need to.

Dr Hassan: So where do you go?

Will: I'm here with you.

Dr. Hassan: And when you leave here?

Will: My work.

Dr. Hassan: Your work.

Will: Yes work. Work is very comforting to me, it keeps things real.

Dr. Hassan: How so?

Will: Accomplishing something important is always a comforting feeling, don't you think?

Dr. Hassan: So when you need comfort you go to your work.

Will: My relationship to my work is the most consistent thing I know.

Dr. Hassan: Not people.

Will: Not people.

Dr. Hassan: And your wife?

Will: What about her?

Dr. Hassan: Do you at all turn to her for comfort?

Will: She knows. I don't have to say a word, women know.

Dr Hassan: How does it feel to be here talking with me?

Will: I think we're wasting time.

Dr. Hassan: I don't Mr. Franklin.

✳

## *He Warrior*

**Once upon a time** there was a boy who wanted to be a warrior and everyday of the year, rain or shine, he would diligently and eagerly climb mountaintops to practice archery and tackle down small beasts. As he grew older and more skillful in his fighting, he yearned to join a clan of warriors and prayed for the day he would go to battle. On his fifteenth year, the fiercest warriors on earth took notice of his martial talents and to his delight, recruited him into their infamous warrior clan. After many years of legendary battles and wars alongside the fierce warriors, the small boy who once tackled down small beasts was awarded the renowned title of He Warrior. He was overjoyed and extremely proud of the honored title and wanted the whole world to speak of his name and fame. His fellow warriors, who were very fond of him, celebrated his earned title by granting him twelve magnificent and memorable full moon feasts where songs were weaved and sung and poems were written and recited in honor of the valiant and fearless He Warrior.

After twelve full moons of eating like a lion, drinking like a hippopotamus and sleeping like a bear, He Warrior finally woke up from his ceremonial stupor howling for action and battle. He placed his shiny metallic armor on his powerful body, polished his mighty and triumphant sword and called for combat. It was said, all on earth who knew of his name and fame were terribly afraid of his brutal force and crushing power. To his horrid surprise, he quickly learned that no one on earth wanted to challenge the great and mighty He Warrior. There was no land left to conquer and no one left to defeat. He Warrior searched and searched for an enemy, any enemy, but there was no enemy in sight to satisfy his thirst for blood and war. With no great challenge to overcome, He Warrior fell into a melancholy state that in short time deepened and deepened into dark gloom and a cruel despair. With no relief in sight, he decided to kill himself and forced an elephant to sit on his unfortunate head. Yuk.

When his spirit journeyed to the other side, a place called Do Little, he was welcomed by a group of old warriors who had prepared a reception feast for him. He was exhilarated and rejoiced that his fame and bravery were honored and celebrated even here in the afterlife land of Do Little. After feasting and much storytelling with the old warriors, his boredom returned and he began asking about possible exploits and battle. The elder warriors laughed and laughed informing him that in this dimension where they are all trapped for a thousand earth years, there were no battles or wars to be fought. He Warrior became mad as a fiery dragon and bellowed at his hosts, but his anger and rage went unanswered by the idle warriors. Deeply frustrated, he went and sat by a still lake and began to throw rocks at the fish contemplating ways of killing himself in order to escape this miserably peaceful place.

An old warrior named Peter approached from the other side of the lake and requested that he stop throwing rocks at the fish. He Warrior briskly stood up and with delight challenged the elder warrior to a duel. The gentle warrior uncontrollably laughed and laughed announcing that in Do Little the bodies of warriors can't be hurt, injured or destroyed. He further explained that only plant and animal life could be hurt, injured or destroyed and advised the young warrior that it would be wise to not hurt, injure or destroy plant and animal life because they are the only things in Do Little that provide the warriors with any sort of activity and purpose. "What bloody purpose?" He Warrior roared. The elder warrior responded calmly and informed him that during their inescapable thousand year stay in Do Little, the purpose of all warriors is to care for all plant and animal life because there is very little else to do, not a thing in fact, nada. After hearing this unhappy news, He Warrior sank into that same unforgiving earthly melancholy and despair and began to mournfully sob. He sobbed and sobbed and inconsolably convulsed like a little orphaned boy. He sobbed from the depths of his being for what seemed a thousand earth years and suddenly for the first time in his adult memory began to feel a twinkle of a need for human comfort. Exhausted in body and mind, he finally grew quiet and fell asleep on the lush meadow along the lake for what seemed an eternity. Peter the old warrior would at times seat himself nearby the sleeping and exhausted young warrior and watch the grass grow. When He Warrior woke up after twelve full moons, the gentle warrior approached him and quietly said, "Do Little is a good place for overzealous warriors like us." He later smiled and gave He Warrior a handful of dead flies and suggested that they feed the hungry fish that were swimming about in the clear water. With meditative pose,

He Warrior flung the dead flies one by one into the still lake and watched the fish jump for their delicious feast.

✳

## Note 3

**"Hello**. Say hello to a good buy and goodbye to your soul." Welcome to the global message in a dysfunctional global economy. How can our boys feel themselves and still remain bonded to their core when they are continuously and strategically targeted as potential consumers and programmed to want-want-want? Our boys came here to serve souls and not our bank and ego accounts. You see, when we throw them off their path at an early age because we want them to buy-buy-buy, we screw up their spiritual wiring. They end up connecting to Exchange Place instead of Mercy Lane. Were boys born with the wiring to consume products without soul? No they were not, they are not. Buy baby buy. Buy this and that and put your soul on layaway and one day you wake up forgetting why on earth you came to earth. *"Check it out. Check out the awwwwesome wheels. Give it a spin and you'll reach the promise land where cooool lives. You know what I mean?"*

So how can he remember, how on earth can any sweet earthly boy remember to stay in the heart, in tenderness, in vulnerability, in faith, in stillness, in purity, in true longing, when his importance is measured as a buyer, a customer, a consumer, a shopper, a purchaser, an end user?

Consumerism has emerged triumphant as the ultimate "ism" on a planet yielding maxed out debts and seriously maxed out male souls who hardly feel they are enough. Is this how we treat each other as souls and then wonder why our next-door neighbor is a white collar criminal, a polluter, an ax murderer? *"That sicko can rot in hell, in hell I say."* That sicko soul was once a child, that sicko soul was once a giant heart dying for love.

No bad boy or bad girl was born bad. The seed of goodness exists in *all* newborns and when this seed is protected and nurtured, acts of mercy and altruism explode. But a sad and tragic thing happened to the life-force and spirit of those so-called bad boys. You know what happened. It happened to me to you and the guy sitting next to you. Emotional deprivation, merciless consumerism and shoulds happened; you know those shoulds that create docile conformity and soul damage. We all know those shoulds that should be silenced. *"I'm goin out tonight to snatch me a Benz, that's right, your Benz."* His precious heart and enoughness were snatched and sold to the highest bidder so now he's gonna snatch your precious Benz so he can feel he is somebody. Greed in men is the product of fear; greed is the product of fear and terror. Shame, embarrassment, vanity, false pride and greed are all products of fear and terror, dig hard enough and you'll see. Greed is a camouflage for fear - the fear of feeling empty way down inside, way down, feeling you're a loser, a reject, not man enough, a nothing because you grew up being told who you are is not enough and is not good enough by Mr. and Mrs. take your pick. You need your greed to feel something, to feel you are real, you are something, you are a man, a somebody. Are you a real man without your hyped symbols and greed? Yes you are, absolutely you are, of course you are. You are your values so please keep telling yourself you're enough without your greed, your unrestrained ambition, and that list of useless desires that aren't worthy of your sacred attention. Change and you'll remember how sweet you once were reciting your ABCs and caressing your blanky. Our lovely boys no longer want to be hostage to an ADD/ADHD hyper-manic post-porn pharmaculture in a GMO landscape steered by the omnipresent and omnipotent GURU-TV. He's driving away with your Benz looking for, looking for his heart, his enoughness, *"I feel cooool in this Benz."* But you are cool and you are enough. There is enough food, enough land, enough alternatives, enough cooperation and enough raw talent to get us out of any trouble and those in power who say there isn't enough are simply not evolved enough and are heavily invested in creating scarcity because it pays off for them. *"I'm comin to get you, your ATM, your Benz, your wife and your life. Yea baby."*

✳

## Will # 3

Will: He rejects my help and whenever I try to open a dialogue he refuses to see or respect my point of view, always an argument. I'm not the enemy I tell him. Do you know what it's like having your son look at you with disdain, with disrespect?

Dr. Hassan: It must hurt.

Will: Like a knife.

Dr. Hassan: This is your middle one?

Will: Yes, Joey.

Dr. Hassan: He must also be in pain.

Will: What do you mean?

Dr. Hassan: You were a son once. Don't you think it's painful for a son to not feel a bond with his father?

Will: I wish he heard you saying that.

Dr. Hassan: What did I say?

Will: His pain about not bonding with me. What does he want? What more does he want from me?

Dr. Hassan: What did you want from your father?

Will: I don't remember. I suppose the same thing, a bond.

Dr. Hassan: Did you get it?

Will: I'm not here to talk about my father.

Dr. Hassan: Did you want to be a lawyer when you were growing up?

Will: Oh yea and I wanted to win. My father was a trial attorney and I could never win an argument with him. It's comical.

Dr. Hassan: What's comical?

Will: He won I lost. The end.

Dr. Hassan: What did he win?

Will: Every argument.

Dr. Hassan: Anything else?

Will: No.

Dr. Hassan: Anything more about your father?

Will: Enough about him. He's not going to help my condition or Joey.

Dr. Hassan: If I asked your son Joey, "what would you change about your father?" what do you think he would say?

Will: Joey's an impractical fool, doesn't yet understand the world, the reality of things, he's an idealist, a romantic. On New Year's Day, New Year's Day of all days and in front of the whole family he attacked me and defended a newspaper article written against me. That was completely unnecessary, way out of line, not on a holiday.

Dr. Hassan: Will, your right hand is shaking.

Will: So?

∗

## Note 4

**Deadness**. Yes that deadness some of us feel because our Light was put out. Maybe our Light was put out in the womb because mom was in a bad funk during her pregnancy. Or maybe the hospital staff and the doctors with all their well-intentioned efforts failed to do the right thing. But more likely life happened. Who in heaven's sake said it's ok to let babies, infants and children cry to sleep? It's definitely absolutely entirely positively not ok. If they cry long enough, hard enough, deep enough, agonizingly enough, they will kill and deaden the need to need you. Here they are showing us their absolute vulnerability, absolute, and we are turning our back because our warrior grandparents and our well meaning but left brained pediatricians told us it's the right thing to do. Well, it's not. It's not ok to prescribe heartbreak because heartbreak will turn inward and kill that part that needs comfort, contact. *"It hurts tooooo much to need. I'll kill and deaden this damn need, I'll put out and turn off my Light."* And when one day that part in them that can still feel empathy is forfeited through consumerism and false desires, the whole planet suffers. Do you know what children do with unmet needs when they grow up? They create chaos for themselves and others. Badness in a kid is a defense, a defense to protect the wounded, broken and terrified heart. Every kid that acts out is acting out because there is a fear, a terror, a freeze, a deeply buried hurt that's driving his energy.

*Fight or flight* from fear and terror. Because our little infant boy bodies couldn't successfully fight fear or take flight from fear, they went into option number three: *Freeze.* When comfort was not provided soon after cold fear entered our little bodies, the fear froze in our cells and paralyzed our movements, speech, actions, thoughts and emotions, in short, our future. Our unfortunate early suffering that overwhelmed and flooded our tender infant and boyhood senses pushed us into defensive amnesia and forced us to forget our histories. Yes, amnesia helped us survive, but we want to live. We want to live in spite of the freeze that prevents us from articulating our hurts and fears into coherent sentences. Yes, we are the brave and not so brave men that you love and want to love who are awkwardly, successfully and unsuccessfully thawing from the deadly freeze.

Children are generally born with a certain amount of Light. You can see it in their movements and you can feel the aliveness of their soul in their eyes. But when they confront controlling, invasive, unfriendly, unresponsive, exploitive, hateful and unfeeling eyes and environments what do you think happens? Day by day the joy gets sucked out and the play is gone. You've seen those kids who can't smile back, like snails retreated so deeply into their shells they can't and you can't feel their spirit. Tragic. Their joy and their play are gone. They decided to go dead in order to survive and the inside mechanism that once playfully and empathically responded to positive stimuli has now shut down like an off switch. The body has survived but large pieces of their soul have floated away to another dimension. Sad. For the rest of their lives they will be living with the pain of not having access to their jump.

So begins their human struggle and desperate search for their joy and their play. So begins their human struggle and journey to reclaim that monumental loss, the loss of their Light, their pieces, their spirit, their aliveness. But because we humans want to feel good fast, we ignore and numb the pain of deadness because we don't ever want to revisit the drama of our tragic history. We men don't like to or want to talk about it. It's common human defense to find an addiction, an obsessive-compulsive replacement, a swap and a trade for our deadness, *"I got to shut down this pain, got to, hurts tooooo much to live like this man, dead, dead inside."* He's got to numb the pain and find a replacement for the lost Light. Replacements are addictions. *"Make me feel good and alive, I want to feel alive man I want to feel alive. I don't want to feel this void in my chest, this empty shell. I got to fill me up with somethin."* Addictions are a distorted search for our salvation, our Light. *"Give me a fix, a chick, a weekend fling, give me my dice, my name, my stocks and fame, give me somethin somethin that'll stop this pain. Give me somethin somethin that'll scream I'm aliiiiiive."* Addicts are a bunch who has found their tragic savior, *"I've found it, I found it baby, I found my savior."* They have found that something to numb the pain of deadness. They have replaced their deadness with a something - a title, a bottle, a needle, a bank account, a fantasy, a sports team, a portfolio, a contemptuous ego, a criminal life, power, more power, control, more control, more sex, more food, more TV, more consumption, more extreme anything. The addict doesn't feel pain; he is saved and feels alive, at least for now. The alcoholic, the rageoholic, the sportsoholic, the sexoholic, the powerholic, the thinkoholic, the workoholic, are all pain free and alive, at least for now.

So how can you heal it, how can we all heal it, how do we replace our socially acceptable and unacceptable addictions, distractions and diversions with authentic and genuine aliveness? Well, we must do the unthinkable. We must do what we have avoided to do, been scared to do, been discouraged to do: We brothers must grieve our monumental loss. We must take a few minutes a day to grieve the loss of our aliveness, our Light, our play, our pieces, our sweetness, our dear boyhood. Few truthful moments a day in the arms of a soulful companion or by a still lake will transform your life, my life. The lost pieces of you and me that reside in that other dimension will return and fill up our partially vacant bodies. The deadness will reduce and your soul will shine inside your darling eyes. Your relationship to yourself, your wife, your partner, your kids, your friends, your enemy, your boss, your coworkers, the trees, your dog and my cat will transform forever.

✳

## Will # 4

Will: Do you know how embarrassing and damaging it would be if my colleagues knew I was seeing you?

Dr. Hassan: Are you suggesting they would perceive you differently?

Will: Damn right.

Dr. Hassan: Is that a scary prospect?

Will: Damn right.

Dr. Hassan: What is scary about it?

Will: What am I doing here? I should be able to solve things on my own.

Dr. Hassan: You're here Will because you can't solve some of the stresses in your life on your own so...

Will: I always did in the past.

Dr. Hassan: There are times when we all need to reach out for help.

Will: I always felt asking for help, comfort, was a humiliating thing because it suggested you're weak, you're a burden to someone.

Dr. Hassan: I'm.

Will: I'm weak.

Dr Hassan: And now?

Will: I must be weak. Look at me, visiting a psychiatrist. I would've never imagined I'd be seeing a shrink.

Dr. Hassan: Your sleep has improved.

Will: A bit.

Dr. Hassan: And your hands are shaking less.

Will: Thanks for the pills.

Dr. Hassan: Who said you're supposed to do it all alone Will?

Will: We did. Somewhere in our makeup there must be a "do it alone" gene.

Dr. Hassan: Or "it's not safe to ask for help" gene.

Will: I suppose.

Dr. Hassan: We don't have to do it alone all the time. I'll see you next week.

*

# PART TWO

# Mercy

*It takes a long time to become young.*

*Pablo Picasso*

## A letter from the boys

To the movers and shakers

Dying of starvation is a brutal thing, brutal. Would you let your kids die of starvation, S-L-O-W-L-Y? How fair is it to destroy food in one country and starve kids in another all in the name of your portfolios. What is with you guys and ladies? Come on already. You're supposed to take care of future generations and our planet but you keep putting profits before people. The purpose of power and wealth according to Einstein and Robin Hood is to help EVERYBODY move forward and be happy. Didn't you all just automatically know what was fair when you were kids? Didn't you all just feel it? You must've. Please take our good advice and heal that gigantic wound in your chests and stop chasing after more power and more money. Heal it already and stop destroying the planet and our future. Enough is enough. What we want you to do is help all lands, all nations, benefiting all souls and not just your small clan.

Hey there Mr. & Ms. Hollywood. You know, with your powerful voices you celebrities can really shut down a lot of bad stuff on this planet. Think about it.

Please don't throw this letter in the shredder and please don't blow it for us.

☺

Your boys

## *Note 5*

**Mer-cy** (mur`se) *noun, plural* -cies. Kind and compassionate treatment of an offender, enemy, prisoner, or other person under one's power; clemency. A disposition to be kind and forgiving. Alleviation of distress; relief. Reprieve from a fate of considerable severity. From Old French *merci*, compassion, forbearance (to someone in one's power), from Late Latin *merces,* reward, God's gratuitous compassion.

**If** I don't have the capacity to feel your need for safety then I am broken and I obliviously live in separation. Because I am broken it is easy for me to break you, scare you, rule you, put out your Light. If you hurt, abuse and exploit others you have very little mercy for yourself. If you dismiss the human race and race to your desk to be number one, you won't find number two. Number two doesn't exist. There is no number two because we're all number one. Life will prove *over and over* that your violent son, your drugged out neighbor, the employee you are exploiting, and that strange stranger who saved your daughter on Route 66 are all number one. The grand illusion that you are number one and I am number two is just that, a monstrous and savage illusion, the greatest lie in the universe. One fine day, the science labs with their priests and priestesses will collapse this fabricated illusion of separation and irrefutably prove that your DNA and mine are wired for mercy. In their white lab coats they will finally conclude that mercy vibrates at a much higher frequency than greed and evil. They will further conclude that mercy, yes, is the most powerful and productive energy in the universe. Worshipping mercy is a good thing, a great thing, because our DNA is made up of lovely particles that delightfully dance in mercy. MERCY RULES.

If you are smarter, stronger, richer and more handsome than I am, let me also know you are more humble. Let me feel safe with you so I won't fear you. My DNA is wired for goodness as well as fear, yes, the fear of disconnection. Your rejection, your condescension, your coldness, your manipulation, your doubletalk, your disdain, your blows, your heartlessness and evil all screw up my wiring. When you humiliate me to feel big, exploit me to get rich, hit me to feel strong, reject me to feel superior, and crush me to feel relief, I don't feel safe. I am wired for mercy and I would appreciate it if you can keep that in mind. Please talk to me when you are in your heart, only when you are in your merciful heart. Did you forget you were once a giant heart in an infant body dying to connect?

Every evil person without exception missed out on mercy, period. Before he hurt anyone, swindled his clients, or hypnotized the masses, the "bad man" had to kill his longing and need to exchange from the heart, a need so deeply buried he has no access to it and can no longer feel his primal innate empathy for you and me. Children who are raised with mercy and people who are treated with mercy don't become dark. His need to steal, lie, exploit, abuse, deny, join gangs, or whatever out of control behavior is presenting itself is there because there is an unattended hurt. Evil didn't grow up witnessing merciful eyes, hearing merciful voices, or feeling the merciful touch of culture. That old repetitious monologue in the head is still screaming: *"Disconnect-disconnect it's not safe to connect, knock em out before they knock me out, yea, I'll connect with my fist and power, yea, that'll teach them mercy."* Evil can only be understood when we understand the darker layers beneath it. Evil is a camouflage, a disguise, a tragic distortion unsuccessfully masking the desperate need for comfort; it is the unfinished business that brews. But evil is *always and always* programmed to self destruct. By its nature, or ill nature, it is always on a collision course because it lives with terror - the terror of opening the heart. But sooner or later, in this life or the next, our hearts are gonna burst open whether we like it or not. Evil is a scary thing, but the terror that creates evil is a lot more scary. If we're not studying how to prevent childhood terror, we're endorsing evil. Still waiting (how long will it take?) for criminal psychologists, sociologists, biologists, judges, lawyers, prosecutors and wardens to enlighten us about the merciless terrors that Wall Street and Main Street criminals grew up with. Why are you professionals holding back and not illuminating us on how a tender little boy becomes a monstrous beast? *"Bull, I don't need you, I don't need nothin from you but your money and your obedience you piece of nothin."*

✳

## *Will # 5*

Will: We've been sleeping in separate bedrooms. This is so unlike Jenny. It's never happened before.

Dr. Hassan: For how long?

Will: Three weeks now.

Dr. Hassan: Did she give a reason?

Will: Her words, "I love you dearly Will but I can't watch you doing this work and continue to respect you."

Dr. Hassan: What does *this work* mean?

Will: Why don't you ask her?

Dr. Hassan: She's not here Will. I'm asking you.

Will: I don't know.

Dr. Hassan: You memorized her words.

Will: You want more? She said and I repeat, "After all these years have you ever considered that some of your critics may have a point?" My critics may have a point? Can you believe this madness? Has she absolutely lost her mind, her senses? My work has paid for our vacations, colleges, her spas and her lunches and now she is questioning her respect for me, my work, my work that paid and pays for everything, unbelievable. She's gone mad I tell you. She actually believes those clowns.

Dr. Hassan: In short, what do your critics seem to be saying?

Will: I'm not here to talk about those idiots.

Dr. Hassan: What do you want to talk about?

Will: My wife.

Dr. Hassan: Will, your hands are shaking again.

Will: So what?

Dr. Hassan: Do you know what Jenny wants from you?

Will: What she wants is for me to abandon my partners.

Dr. Hassan: You mean to quit the firm?

Will: Yes.

Dr. Hassan: Why do you use the word abandon?

Will: Because that's what she's asking me to do.

Dr. Hassan: And you don't want to abandon your partners.

Will: No I don't.

Dr. Hassan: Abandoning them will make you feel what?

Will: It's not an option.

Dr. Hassan: Are you feeling more scared than angry?

Will: I want her back. I want things to be the same.

Dr. Hassan: Are you scared of losing her?

Will: I want things to be the same.

Dr. Hassan: Do you observe her to be changing?

Will: Changing?

Dr. Hassan: Her views, her priorities, are they changing?

Will: After thirty-eight years of marriage?

Dr. Hassan: People do change Will. What's important right now is how you are being affected by her changes and her words.

Will: Well, you can see how I'm being affected.

Dr. Hassan: Yes I can. We'll work on reducing your fears about this and see if you and your wife can negotiate your differences.

Will: I'm angry not afraid. And what's there to negotiate?

Dr. Hassan: We'll find out together. You don't feel any fear around this issue?

Will: Life would be hard without her, very hard.
Dr. Hassan: One step at a time Will.

✱

## Note 6

**The** opposite of love is not hate, indifference, or anything that has to do with aggression. The opposite of love is loss of faith and a sentence to a life of fear and terror. When you peel the layers of hate, indifference and aggression, what you find is fear and terror, fear and terror from something. The greatest fear and terror is the terror of disconnection, separation, rejection, abandonment. We are wired for mercy and connection and anything that threatens that wiring sends us boys and men into paranoid withdrawal or unabashed aggression or somewhere in-between. If we're not talking about fear, we're not talking. Fear. It runs us, dominates our thoughts and will only change when we create safety. Safety, safety. The remedy for fear is safety and you can correct me if I'm wrong but correct me only if you're in your warm heart because it's very difficult to hear and absorb what you're saying when I don't feel safe with you. You understand me don't you, you get what I'm sayin? Turns out deep inside we're all looking for the same precious commodity in human exchange: Safety, a byproduct of mercy.

Another byproduct of mercy is faith, and if you think and feel like a boy who has not been deprived of mercy you will have full possession of your faith, your four faiths: Faith in yourself, faith in humanity, faith in tomorrow, and faith in God. Yes God because you've got to believe there is a force out there and in here in our masculine hearts that *is* running the show. A sperm and an egg come together and create a fetus, a life, a child, a human boy or girl. That is one gigantic massive gargantuan colossal miracle that has got to burst your heart open and humble you down to your knees. There's got to be a God. God is Mercy and Mercy is God. Amen to that! So where was God when evil was carrying out its dark deeds? Well, that's the history of our human free will gone amok. If faith in ourselves, in human cooperation, in tomorrow and in God runs us, then fear won't run the show. The more there is faith the less the volume of fear, the more there is faith, the stronger the sweet and reassuring feeling of safety. Our boys are born with faith in themselves and never think of themselves as weak or stupid or ugly, at least not until the outside world bombards them with disapproval that sets in the long term damage.

Do you think boys feel safe enough to keep their tender hearts open in school and walk around with their chest exposed screaming "I love my sweetness?" The unfortunate answer and truth is no. Daily they go to school with armored hearts and remain armored until graduation, God knows what happens after graduation. The schools have become a twelve year broken heart sentence for our boys. How can a sweet schoolboy develop and build up his nerves and muscles of faith and self-love when he feels scared, less than, inferior, not enough? Our boys need emotional safety and faith, yes, faith in their adults Mr. Education, so will you fight for them? Remember Mr. Education, how a long time ago, in your crib, your playpen, and in your schoolyard your fear howled and cried *"don't put out my Light,"* remember? If you don't remember then you can't fully know what your boys need and what your responsibility is. We men must all remember our pain from being scared and terrified and how our faith in ourselves got sucked out of our small lungs. You and I must remember our fear of alienation, humiliation, and deprivation, to name a few. Those fears captured in the B&W and fading color photos collecting dust in the attic and basement. Clear the dust and look. Please look and acknowledge the loss of your sweetness so you can begin to see your story, my story, the male story. When you and I remember our full narrative, then our robust free will is ready to guide, help, serve and heal the boys. From the history of our fears, terrors, pain and goodness comes the boys' salvation. So remember, because it is our divine act of remembering that will save our divine boys from future misfortune.

If you think and feel like a boy who has not been deprived of mercy you will easily know how to fix the world, really. You and I are more intelligent than most children but I believe they are wiser. They, these amazing children of ours are wiser because their approach to problem solving is anchored in *connecting*, not separating. These numinous beings entered earth to serve the "we consciousness" because they know it's not only about the "me." Without knowing it, these kids are beyond the separating nature of religion, language, culture and race. They sense and feel what is similar in us much more than what is different.

Their innate inborn cellular wiring is holy and their DNA is designed for connection. They are born theologians hooked up to the heavens and have access to a data of information that we forgot, but they still remember. They can tell us what the soul is and why it exists and some will even tell you why all the pain and evil. Connecting, that is their sacred mission, connecting you to me. Because they haven't forgotten, they qualify as our teachers. They can effortlessly walk the walk and talk the talk if we would just let them, let them *be* instead of do do do, buy buy buy. Spirituality is the courage to initiate actions that reduce separation and promote connections among people. Our boys yearn and long for experiences that help them remain connected to their sacred mission and to the full spectrum of their emotions and yes they want to live on a spiritual planet that reduces terror and spreads mercy. But most are scared and terrified and some are angry, very angry. They are angry because they are hurt. They are angry because they are deeply hurt. They are hurt because we do not support their wiring for mercy. They are deeply hurt because we do not...

✳

## Will # 6

Will: He found out I am seeing you and asked Jenny about it.

Dr. Hassan: You mean Joey found out?

Will: Who else do you think I'm talking about?

Dr. Hassan: Are you angry with me?

Will: You think I want to be here?

Dr Hassan: Are you angry because you don't want to be here?

Will: Didn't I just say that?

Dr. Hassan: Why else are you angry?

Will: Does there have to be anything else?

Dr. Hassan: Do you think I'm a good listener?

Will: No, not really. You didn't realize it was Joey I was talking about.

Dr. Hassan: Are you angry because you had to repeat yourself to me, because you didn't feel understood or heard?

Will: Try to follow me.

Dr. Hassan: I'll do my best.

Will: Good.

Dr. Hassan: Where does it hurt you when you feel that you're not being understood or heard?

Will: Where?

Dr. Hassan: Yes where in your body does it ache, hurt?

Will: Uh, my head.

Dr. Hassan: What does your head need in order to feel better, to feel relief?

Will: It needs you to shut up.

Dr. Hassan: I won't speak Will.

Will: Good. Nobody hears me anyway, nobody. I'm always repeating myself. Don't you listen, doesn't anyone listen? Oh my head just wants to explode.

*

# Note 7

**In** our global village, Spiritual Leaders need to step up and live up to their calling as Mercy Leaders. You can't possibly say you have faith in God when you lack mercy. Spiritual faith without mercy is a contradiction, an impossibility. Spirituality is the doctrine of merciful and humble service. The most holy and sacred act by anyone who is in power is to serve with mercy and not abuse power. When we serve others we serve ourselves. That which we want to receive we must learn to give. Lead with mercy and be a Mercy Leader. Yes, MERCY LEADER. Don't you like that title more than that abstract and intangible job title of Spiritual Leader? We the people like that a lot because that title is simple and it says all that needs to be said about spirituality. The task of a Mercy Leader is to spread mercy and reduce terror, simple. We the people and the suffering underdogs love simple; we don't need to spin simple into complex. Simple is functional, practical, and we desperately need functional-practical spirituality that above all else worships mercy.

If children and women of religion X are starving to death or being hacked to pieces, what is your responsibility as the leader of religion Y? Will your mercy dictate and make a holy decision? If your religion separates you from the bloodbath of others then your wiring for mercy has collapsed and will sink us deeper into that black hole, it will. Anyone and everyone who is a leader in every little and big corner of the world has an obligation and an opportunity to be a Mercy Leader. *"I have a dream that one day that seed of mercy in you and in me will bloom like a giant May flower and we'll all worship mercy cause mercy revolution's comin to town."* Because no boy was born a criminal, a sadist, a pervert, or a dictator, it is the absolute responsibility of all leaders, absolute, to nurture and protect the seed of mercy born in all newborns, not only locally but also globally. MERCY RULES.

God is merciful and merciful is God is written in the scriptures of all religions. Their primary message is reduce terror and spread mercy. Good message, Holy message, thank you dear messengers, let's move on. Without it, mercy that is, the planet is shot, over, kaput; you know that, I know that, Gandhi, Thurgood Marshall and Lady Diana knew that, and Mr. Mandela who joins that rank of Mercy Leaders certainly knows that. When I'm in your power what will you do with me? When a hundred million people and their forests are in your power will you show mercy? The function and purpose of power is to serve and not self-serve. If you are rich and powerful (or a parent), your most important responsibility, duty, service, obligation and commitment is to spread mercy. You and I were born to spread mercy, everything else is a footnote.

Acts of worship that doesn't include prayer for the entire globe slows down your evolution and mine. If I want my dreams to come true, I must pray for the world, not only for my tribe, my town and my street. Our prayer must extend beyond language, race, color, village and country, dear brothers. We must all learn to be global praying citizens. East must pray for west, west must pray for south, south must pray for north, and north must pray for... Prayer can no longer remain local; it's got to go global with one primary message: Reduce terror and spread mercy, all else is secondary chant. *What do we want? Mercy. When do we want it? Now.*

Is it not the responsibility of Spiritual Leaders to defend and secure the basic material needs and innate rights of their followers? Of course it is. The bare bone interests of the preacher's flock are directly connected to the realities of economic, social, political and environmental policies. Every every policy out there is a moral issue. There is no policy out there that does not have moral implications, none. Can you call yourself a Spiritual Leader and remain apolitical, is that possibly possible? *"Got to protect and water that seed and Preacher you got to step up."* Is it not the role of a Spiritual Leader, sorry, Mercy Leader, to reduce terror wherever he sees it, feels it in his bones and smells it? You bet. *"We're praying Mr. Preacher that policymakers be merciful and that you, yes you, help with your voice cause we're waitin on you and we've had enough."* By remaining apolitical are you not contributing to injustice and is not your spirituality a mask, a respectable job without soul? *"So let's hear your mighty Preacher heart scream and shout: 'Have mercy for justice'."*

Help Wanted: Global Mercy Leaders (GMLs)
Mercycore is expanding its global operations and immediately hiring 754,000 more GMLs. Perfect time for

mission possible. Perfect time for Mercy Leaders to go global, like Coke and Pepsi. Must be excellent investigator and collector of facts. Must possess a degree in Ethics, have conscience, courage, and passionately worship mercy. Must know how to step up, speak up, scream and shout in the name of mercy. Great salary with 6 week paid vacation a year. Housing, healthy food (no pesticides, insecticides, hormones, fillers, additives, coloring, and antibiotics), healthcare package and silent retreats all included along with abundant emotional benefits. Travel to hot spots to reduce terror and spread mercy. Travel and work with exceptionally evolved men and women (*you may even meet your soul mate - 232,258 matches to date*). Send e-mail to: GML@saveus.heart

✳

## *Superhero*

**What** makes a boy a man and what makes a man a hero? The national soul of a country is defined by its heroes. So who are the modern day heroes (or anti-heroes) of our young boys and girls? Heroes set into motion certain attitudes and beliefs that eventually become part of our cultural mythology and cellular memory. Through their stories, heroes shape traditions and define adulthood to the young; therefore, we adults must pay extra-extra careful attention to our children's heroes. The heroes they choose influence and guide their decisions for years to come. The parent, the teacher and the mayor, must all know who their children's heroes are and what those heroes are saying about mercy and what makes a boy a man and a girl a woman. Not all heroes are good heroes. False heroes are those who push for disconnection because they perversely benefit from the walls of division. Heroes can either foster connection or sponsor separation; like knives, they can either cut birthday cakes or cut up and obliterate childhood innocence. Whether you know it or not, accept it or not, you and I are always a hero to our boys because we exist. I exist therefore I am a hero. The banker, the baker, the computer-chip maker can either contribute Light or lead us deeper into the abyss. So let's be great heroes guys with great stories to tell to our boys.

Below is "The Eightfold Path" which outlines the list of the eight fundamental, critical and indispensable values and codes of conduct which qualify men as modern day heroes. If your hero is violating "The Eightfold Path," time to bump him off and find a new hero.

1 - The modern day hero will leave behind the least possible amount of carbon footprints.

2 - The modern day hero is convinced that kids are his soulful teachers.

3 - It is easy for the modern day hero to say, "Oops, I made a mistake, very sorry, please forgive me, I'll learn from this one."

4 - The modern day hero does not tolerate abuse and exploitation in his community and workplace and fights to eradicate it.

5 - The modern day hero does not take advantage of weaker men because in his blood he feels that all men are his brothers.

6 - The modern day hero does not exploit women because he respects the "Wise Woman" in all women.

7 - The modern day hero believes that all is connected and that separation is illusion.

8 - The modern day hero's mission is to help others evolve toward mercy and joy.

9 - (Optional) The modern day hero is humorous and likes to make people laugh without laughing at people.

∗

## Will # 7

Will: So in order for us to stay together I must hear what she has to say even if I disagree with her.

Dr. Hassan: Exactly. That's the effective way to negotiate. You must hear her out Will. In true dialogue, both sides have to be willing to change.

Will: Hope it works.

Dr. Hassan: How is the punching bag coming along?

Will: I love it. Better to punch a bag than tear someone's head off.

Dr. Hassan: Sure is. What does tearing someone's head off mean?

Will: Exactly what it says.

Dr. Hassan: Help me understand that better.

Will: It's not important.

Dr. Hassan: The punching bag is helping you discharge what?

Will: Frustration, anger.

Dr. Hassan: Good.

Will: I'm aware of my hands a lot.

Dr. Hassan: What do your hands want to do, express?

Will: They're on fire. They want to choke, choke you, choke someone.

Dr. Hassan: That's a lot of anger Will.

Will: Lot of rage. It scares me sometimes; it scares Jenny.

Dr. Hassan: I'm sure it does. If the rage could speak, what would it say?

Will: You don't want to know.

Dr. Hassan: Try me Will.

Will: Forget it.

Dr. Hassan: Where else in your body do you feel the anger, the rage.

Will: In my head. My head wants to scream. I just want to scream, explode.

Dr. Hassan: At whom, at what? What would you say?

Will: I can't do this.

Dr. Hassan: It's safe here Will.

Will: I can't do it.

Dr. Hassan: Ok. What do you think is under all the rage Will?

Will: I don't know, more rage. You tell me, no, I don't want to know.

Dr. Hassan: Do you have an intuitive sense about it?

Will: I'm not a psychiatrist Doc.

Dr. Hassan: I know you're not but you must have an intuitive sense about your health. You couldn't have been this successful in your profession without an intuitive sense. Will you do an exercise with me?

Will: Maybe.

Dr. Hassan: Let's bring your attention, your focus, out of your head and to your body. Can you do that?

Will: I'll try.

Dr. Hassan: Put your hands on your stomach. Now try to bring your focus down to where your hands are. Just drop your attention down into your belly and try to stay there. Don't go back up to your head. Keep the focus down. That's great Will. How does it feel to be there instead of your head?

Will: Uh, less busy.

Dr. Hassan: That's good Will. I want you to do this at home for ten minutes a day please.

Will: And you think this helps?

Dr. Hassan: Yes I do. After all, feelings are felt in our body, aren't they? I want you to remember that under the anger, the hurt, the rage, and the fear is joy. What we're trying to do is get to the joy but we got some mud to go through first. Do you understand?

Will: Not really but I'll give it a shot.

Dr. Hassan: Good. Please try to do the exercise ten minutes a day and we'll catch up next week.

✳

## Note 8

**Listening.** So much noise around me and inside me. I have to be silent to hear myself, my truth, my wanting, my inner guidance, my instincts, my soul's purpose. Silence, what luxury! I must afford myself this luxury of silence. God and the voice of innocent children speak when I am silent and still. I can only hear them when I am silent and still. Yes to silence and stillness. When I listen I hear and sense the message, the inner guidance, and then I know which door to knock. I listen and then take action. There is always the right door. There is always enough. If a door doesn't open there is another, there is. There are always options. It's not cool breaking down doors that aren't opening, that's not wisdom.

No. The no thing. I give you permission to say no. Say no to me if you must, if the signals, sounds, messages and voice of your silent and still body are saying no. You can reject my demands, but don't reject the demands and voice of your wise male core. Your male core with its wise instincts is the pilot, not my needs, wants, requests and demands. Say yes to you, to your gut feelings and instincts. You deserve to fight for your no and say yes to yourself, to your wise man. What do my demands know compared to the wisdom of your stillness? Your inner being has spoken, please listen, lisssen. You can say no to me if you must. Say no without guilt, without anxiety, without shame and despair. Whether you know it or not, I'm in the hands and in the care of Life's Pulse and you are free.

Please stop giving without resting. Every car has to stop to refuel sooner or later and every burned out compassionate soul has to rest at one point. Rest your head and let the gods revitalize your body and mind. The god of rest, the god of tranquility, and the god of silence are all here and excited to help. Give when you are ready to give, prepared to give, have enough energy, money and skill to give. Do you know when to stop giving? Do you give to everyone who asks, do you give when you shouldn't? If I am continually refusing your help, pray for me, walk away and go home. You've done the best you can, you've given enough, you are enough.

Give to me from your compassion as well as your detachment. Please remain detached from my pain, you don't own it and you don't have to. Don't absorb my pain into your skin and into your cells. Hold the boundary and don't lose yourself in my pain, stay inside your skin and cells. Make sure you can feel yourself when you are helping me or else you are lost, lost. Take a break, walk away and find yourself, find you, find your interior. Take a deep breath and be glad you still have a skin that separates you from me. If you know what I need, do you know what you need? If you know what I want, do you know what you want? I hope you do because I don't want your needs and wants on the back burner. If you place my needs and wants on the front burner you will resent me someday, you will. So please don't lose your needs and wants on my account. Your core will tell you when to stop giving, please listen. It will post a STOP sign for you so you may comply. It will tell you who to give to and yes who to not give to, please listen. Listen well to the signals, sounds, messages and voice of this wise body before you burn it out. STOP means you are off duty and higher powers are in charge.

Do you take when others give? Can you receive and take when it is given to you? What every man wants from another man is strength and vulnerability. If you are always strong to the degree that your vulnerability is invisible, life will one day place you on your humble knees. If you are always vulnerable to the degree where your strength is invisible, please ask for help, receive, and get bold. Do you shy away from receiving maybe because receiving turns up the fear? Have you learned to take and surrender to another's giving? Oh surrender, that surrender thing, not being in control, fearing surrender, fear of surrender. Control is a thousand dollar word for fear, you know that. *"I got to control cause I'm scared, afraid, not safe. If I control I'm in control, I'm safe, no terror."* You strip away the control and fear is lurking below. If I surrender to your giving then you're in control. *"If I surrender to your giving will you line up a list of conditions and trap me? If I surrender to your giving will you betray me?"* Do you remember when we opened our tender boy hearts and surrendered?

But the purpose, the purpose of listening, saying no, saying yes to our male core, giving, receiving, and surrendering, is to connect, to bond, to belong, to feel joy and meaning, to feel acknowledged, validated, to feel anchored, grounded and rooted. Listening, saying no, saying yes to me, connecting, belonging, rooting, Amen!

*

# *The king who could not laugh*

**Once upon a time** there was a king whose greatest ambition was to possess the entire wisdom of the universe. He surrounded himself daily with the greatest of poets, the wisest of judges, and the finest of scholars. With insatiable hunger, this king read all the books the libraries of his kingdom had to offer and memorized the cleverest of sonnets and poems. He was indeed a man of great knowledge but insisted that his true passion lay in the study of wisdom. He would often make a distinction between the two by asserting to his court that knowledge was the accumulation of acquired memory, but in wisdom rested the fruit of experience that would endlessly enrich one's soul. Because he felt his fruit was still green and unripe, his search for scholarly adventures and ever-larger volumes of penetrating books continued to consume his life.

In the late hours of one dark night the king was awakened by an incredible dream unaware that it would someday become his curse. He jumped out of bed and immediately called his court to a late night session. The members of the court walked in with their slumberous strides and sat down obediently wondering why they were called by their king at such a late hour. The king cleared his throat, spoke to them with vigor, and said, "Tonight, I had a dream, no, a revelation which has restored me with strength and purpose. Once in a lifetime comes a dream from the night that charts a king's purpose and mission. I have been blessed with such a dream my dear members of the court. As you all know, for many years I have been searching for wisdom and I admit to you with genuine frustration that I have not found it. Tomorrow, I will prepare to march with my three sons and my army to all the lands and seas as far as the eye can see to satisfy my desire for wisdom." Members of the king's court looked at one another in confusion as the king continued. "In my dream tonight, I saw a human being like you and I bleeding in a color other than our own. His skin was not leaking the red liquid blood that we are all unfortunately too familiar with; but rather, he was bleeding in gold, in the color gold. From his skin was running a liquid unlike anything the world has seen. The color gold was flowing and glowing from his body." Staring at his court with crazed eyes, the king declared, "I see it so clearly now, another human species must exist that we have not yet met. There must be another race of humans living under our skies who do not bleed in red. I must find them. We must find these humans who might, no, who will enlighten us. I believe they will answer the questions the poets have failed to answer, you have failed to answer. This dream has indeed given me hope and direction. Prepare the army for departure and call forth my sons. We *will* find these humans."

Members of the court were astonished and horrified. It was one thing to be consumed by a fantastic dream, but to mobilize an army was pure madness. They decided to not challenge the king's delusional state during an obvious manic episode and agreed to wait for sunrise. They secretly believed the king had become insane yielding to a devilish dream and prayed that the morning sun would restore his senses and reason.

Well, it did not. The following week, against the advice of the baffled court and his queen, the king advanced his mighty army with his three sons and headed to lands and seas as far as the eye can see. North, south, east and west, the iron willed king was determined to find humans with golden blood and secure the wisdom of the universe. But as all had greatly feared and foreseen, the king's mad and extensive quest had reduced the large army to a fraction. Savage tribes, unforgiving winters, heat, hunger, dehydration and exhaustion, had sadly claimed the lives of thousands of soldiers as well as the lives of the king's beloved three sons. The famous king had traveled the four-corners of the earth for two decades and had failed to realize his dream, a dream that now roused within him rage and immense grief.

Upon his return, the dejected king solemnly handed the queen the decomposed bodies of their three sons and without a word to his court or to his subjects, retreated to his private quarters, closed the iron doors of all his rooms and as the story tells, remained in seclusion for a span of seven long years. It was rumored that infrequently he would accept food and water only if given to him by his mourning queen. In his self-imposed isolation, his darkened heart was inconsolable; and oftentimes, in the black of the night, one could hear through the stone walls of the great palace his cries of sorrow, and the curses bellowing at the sky, the gods, and his seductive dream.

One spring morning, the king emerged from his dark quarters and called his queen, his court, his poets, his judges and his scholars to assembly. All were very happy to learn their king was breaking his silence and were eager to hear what he would announce after an absence of seven years. When all were gathered, he quietly began to speak and said, "I have been wandering in my quarters for years now in lamentation, bitterness and rage. I have found it impossible to recover from my ruin, which as you all know has been enormous. You have all said to learn from mistakes is wisdom and yes, I have learned much from my mistakes. But what good is all this learning if I can not laugh. I am always with my grief, a grief that leaves no room for joy. I have become this wretched old man who can not smile a note. Is my smile buried in order to protect me from future calamity and pain? I asked to see you today to inform you that I have finally discovered what wisdom is; yes, it is the ability and the strength to suffer misfortune and still feel joy, to suffer calamity and still feel the heart that wants to exchange a few words and a few laughs. So you are here today to help me not find wisdom but laughter. I now clearly see that wisdom is this human hurdle - to live tragedy and remain tender, to live tragedy and still laugh. Have any of you lived a tragedy with all its darkness and still remained accessible? Those who have, I want to hear from you. You may now all leave."

The poets, the judges, the scholars and members of the court walked out quietly pondering upon the king's words. As for the king, he slowly marched to the queen's quarters carrying a handful of fresh figs wrapped in silk and timidly announced his presence. She appeared at the gate and stood before him in her elegance and silence. He tenderly handed her the fruit and invited her for a stroll to the rose garden. To his surprise, she extended her graceful hand and accepted the long awaited invitation with a warm smile.

✳

## Will # 8

Dr. Hassan: Did you speak to your partners?
Will: I'm not ready to do that yet.
Dr. Hassan: We'll go at your pace Will.
Will: Thanks.
Dr. Hassan: You're welcome.
Will: Once I retire I think I want to let Jenny guide the course more.
Dr. Hassan: Have you told her that.
Will: I have, indirectly.
Dr. Hassan: Good.
Will: I feel I am less in my head today.
Dr Hassan: Do you like that?
Will: Less electricity and rage up there.
Dr. Hassan: What can you do to maintain and support that?
Will: I don't know.
Dr. Hassan: What helps you relax, slow down, contract?

Will: My horse Luke, Chaplin movies, vacations with Jenny.

Dr. Hassan: That's great. Keep up with the belly exercises please. Is there a vacation on the horizon?

Will: She's planning one.

Dr. Hassan: Good. So what was it that happened at work?

Will: I'm swimming with this sentence I overheard; I still feel it in my body.

Dr. Hassan: Do you want to tell me?

Will: I don't know... It all sounds silly now. I walked into my office last Thursday morning and one of my receptionists was on the phone. She didn't hear me come in and she was going on and on and at one point she said, "My older sister didn't cry a tear."

Dr. Hassan: Yes.

Will: At that very moment I wanted to annihilate her. I immediately asked my assistant Karen to have her fired for good. I just couldn't listen to that voice again. I realize now I was killing the messenger.

Dr. Hassan: The messenger who said, "My older sister didn't cry a tear."

Will: Yes.

Dr. Hassan: What's revealing about that line?

Will: It hit me; hit me hard. It made me panic.

Dr. Hassan: So that sentence scared you?

Will: I suppose. It made my hands shake but I didn't want to beat up anyone.

Dr. Hassan: That's good. Were you feeling more fear than anger?

Will: I suppose, yes.

Dr. Hassan: So the sentence scared you.

Will: Yes. I think I know what Joey wants from me. It's what I wanted when I was growing up. I think I was about six and had this fantasy that tears were the opposite of steel, that wet tears would soften steel, melt it down. I remember drawing that in my art class. I remember wanting and wishing the earth would open up and swallow everyone so that they would cry, so that they would be forced to cry. I drew all that. All the adults around me were like steel, a wall of solid resistance I couldn't budge, including my older sister.

Dr. Hassan: And if they were forced to cry what would happen?

Will: Then I could cry. I would have permission to cry.

Dr. Hassan: What would you have cried about?

Will: I really don't know Doc.

Dr. Hassan: You must have been a very perceptive child to sense all that and draw it. Have you kept the drawings?

Will: I burned them all when my mother died. I didn't cry when she died.

Dr. Hassan: You were eleven.

Will: Yes.

Dr. Hassan: Was she buried or cremated?

Will: Buried in Virginia.

Dr. Hassan: When did you last visit her?

Will: Fourteen years ago.

Dr. Hassan: You said you know what your son Joey wants from you.

Will: My son, he wants to dent my steel and watch me cry.
Funny how it all circles.

Dr. Hassan: Yes. So Joey wants the same thing you wanted
when you were growing up. You wanted to melt the steel
in your family and he wants to dent and soften your steel.
Is that close?

Will: I think so. Yes.

Dr. Hassan: It sounds like he's mirroring an important
part of you, a forgotten and missing part of you.

Will: What do you mean?

Dr. Hassan: The part of you that abandoned your tears and
your desire to speak from the hurt.

Will: I suppose.

Dr. Hassan: How do you feel about what Joey wants from
you?

Will: Can you believe it makes me want to cry?

Dr. Hassan: You have permission here Will.

✳

## Found

**You** can cheat, steal, conspire, manipulate and corruptly
rise to great power and you will still be at the beginning
of your journey and will not reach the end, whatever the
end means to you. The end for most of us is that far away
nursing home with three unfortunate meals a day followed
by an afterlife where we'll all have to make amends. You
and I can't reach our end when we haven't yet begun our

beginning, when we haven't yet considered our evolution, that is - we haven't yet challenged our flawed personality to live by the rules of our soul. Our personality incarnated to be purified and to match the depth and wisdom of our sacred soul. It incarnated to begin a journey, our human journey; it incarnated to accumulate the riches and powers of our male mercy.

For thousands of years the primary spiritual message has been the same: Reduce terror and spread mercy. The most powerful, the most refined and the most holy of acts is mercy because the pulse of our planet is measured by mercy as well as by the unfortunate absence of mercy. Our spirituality and divinity is ultimately measured by the amount of mercy that bathes our bloodstream. Leaders will convene in a thousand more global conferences on social, environmental, political, labor and economic strategies and prescriptions, but it is yes mercy that will save the world. It is the divine act of mercy that will transform fear to love and drain the terror from our bodies. And when this alien entity is finally drained we will not steal, hoard or kill anymore because we will no longer be propelled by the darkness of our childhood and adult terrors.

Mercy starts at home. Mercy to me. Be merciful enough to give to me, to myself. Give to myself praise for the things I do right. Give to myself patience with myself. Give to myself direction, guidance, purpose and mission. Give to myself healthy friendships. Give to myself hope, faith, courage and optimism. Mercy is a good thing because you got to have mercy for yourself to get out of a lousy relationship, a lousy job or a lousy neighborhood. But pray for and bless the lousy things you leave behind because they made you humble and strong. Give to myself nurturing. Nurturing myself means to trust my intuition, to give without losing myself, to Seek Divine Wealth, to finish school and to love without smothering the object of love. It further means to stop smoking, to pursue, to fight, to speak up, to not fight, to meditate, to not exploit, to listen, to talk less, to let go, to be still, to eat right, to ask for directions, to sob, to rebel, to be thankful, to work with enthusiasm, to laugh, to play and to pray for the higher good. I must have enough mercy for myself to not deny myself my deep longings and calling. Have enough mercy for myself to step up and be the primary storyteller to my son and protect my son from storytellers with profiteering motives. Have enough mercy to forgive myself for my wrongdoings and for all those decisions I once made that screwed things up. Mr. & Mrs. Mercy forgive us and clear us from all the mess we men have made as long as, as long as, we move towards mercy and self-mercy. We can't teach mercy to others if we can't give it to ourselves.

Our soul is boundless mercy and when our flawed personality decides to match the breath, depth, and power of our soul, we have begun our beginning. We can follow the will of our personality for however long we want but sooner or centuries later after we have exhausted every whim and fancy of our personality, our soul will be there waiting for us in ceremony. In a moving reunion it will envelop all of our male history in mercy and welcome us with open arms. It will celebrate our return with tears and announce how much we were missed. It will forgive every injury we suffered and caused and hold us in tender embrace. Alas, all that was dark will turn to Light and we will no longer feel lost. What was lost was our purpose and now it is found. We have found why we incarnated upon this earth, our Earth, with its torment and breathtaking beauty, with its Wounded Knee and Grand Canyon, its Bhopal and Mount Everest. Alas, we have found our purpose and Heaven is pleased. Now that we have found our purpose, we, bold, powerful and gentle men, can roll up our sleeves and begin our beginning; we can begin to mercifully extinguish the legacy of terror on our magnificent planet.

One day we will open ourselves up to mercy because at the core, mercy IS who we are, and none of us can forever escape and hide from who we truly are. After we have lived through every addiction and habit, abused and been abused, we will inevitably search for mercy and find it. WE WILL FIND IT. We will definitely, absolutely, unequivocally find it. It could take five minutes, five years or fifty more lifetimes, but one day, one fine day, one promised blessed day, we men will stand before each other and embrace the merciful thing that we all are and cheerfully whisper hello.

## *The Beginning*

# Afterword: Resources

For men to be better fathers, brothers, sons, community, political and spiritual leaders, a combination of individual inner work as well as brave group is needed to increase awareness. Admittedly, the "awareness work" for men is still in development but more men's groups and seminars are becoming available and entering mainstream. Through such groups and seminars, men are forming "communities" where they can go for support and guidance without feeling judged or criticized. Men's groups can create opportunities for men to safely "parent and father" each other and connect to deeper feelings and power.

"The Masculine Heart" seminars which I conduct are mainly about creating an environment where we men can feel safe enough to blossom into our truth and step away from untruth and unawareness.

You can start your own "Men's Support Group" in your home, business, or community and carry out readings of this book and or the books listed below. There are more books about men that can be found through an internet search.

"The Hero with a Thousand Faces" by Joseph Campbell

"Fire in the belly: on being a man" by Sam Keen
"King, Warrior, Magician, Lover" by Robert Moore and Douglas Gillette
"Iron John" by Robert Bly
"Living the Truth" by Keith Ablow MD
"The Anger Solution' by John Lee

Below is a list of men's groups as well as support groups from Google search.

www.mkp.org - The mankind project
www.menstuff.org
www.johnleebooks.com
12 Step Programs
Religious Organizations
Youth Organizations

You can also go to my website www.drrobertkandarjian.com and click "Resources" where you will find a list of educational and healing centers where seminars for men are available.

# Notes

# Notes

# Notes

# Notes

# Notes